FIND ANSWERS
WITHIN

VINISHA MARKAN

INDIA • SINGAPORE • MALAYSIA

ISBN 979-8-89133-623-0

Acknowledgments

I thank my mother for making me the person I am today. You have given me the strength that I have today. Despite of so many struggles, you ensured, your children are able to dream big and have a lot of warmth in their hearts.

You inspire me in all ways possible.

About the Book

This book is a deep spiritual work brought together exclusively for you. If you have got your hand on it, it is meant for you.

Believe in that and let the magic begin.

In the times of being lost, when you aren't able to find a way through or are not wanting to talk to someone, this book is going to be your best friend. Because, everything lies within you.

Yes, the answers to all our questions are within us and this book has been written to help you find them.

How to use the book to provide you the best:

- Keep the book in your hands
- Take a deep breath
- Close your eyes.
- Think about a question or the thought which is bothering you.
- Now, open your eyes and randomly pick a page from the book.
- Open it, and that's your Answer Key.
- Read it, reflect on it and pay gratitude towards everything you are blessed with.

It's important to keep moving. No matter how hard the struggle is, you need to keep going. Walk, crawl, no matter how slow, but don't stop. You will reach your goal.

Why are you apprehensive? What is stopping you? Trust your intuition and take that risk. Surrender the apprehension. You are almost there.

ALCHEMY

Miracles are everywhere. Inside you, outside of you, everywhere. You, yourself are a miracle. Just be patient, be alert to receive the miracle. You are blessed.

Have faith. Having faith in itself is a step towards accomplishment and victory. If you have faith in yourself and the divine, there is no one who can stop you from achieving, even the unachievable.

Keep your heart warm, even towards who hurt you. Let them hurt you, they are ignorant and cold. You don't be that. You are not doing this to prove yourself to anyone but to have your own peace. The warmer your heart is, the better your breathing is.

Be grateful. Look around and see so many are less fortunate. Not just in terms of material things but even relationships. There are few who don't have anyone who is there to make them feel loved. Close your eyes and feel the love and abundance you have in your life. Count your blessings.

Help someone today. Be a hand of happiness. Find someone around who can feel happy by your act of generosity. But don't be proud of yourself. Don't donate used items, buy something new for someone today. Feel the happiness double up.

Speak to someone you haven't spoken for a while. Tell them that you still love them and how you miss them. Rejuvenate yourself today with the enthusiasm of invoking a dormant yet an important relationship.

Detox, you need to cleanse your gut. Make fasting once a while, a regular practice. For now, have some fresh fruit, salad, juice or a soup for the rest of the day. Enjoy a beautiful sleep.

Pause. Where are you running? What is it that you want to achieve? Slow down, switch on the pause button for now. You have been running around a little too much. You have exhausted yourself. Pause now before your body forces you to.

When you grow your life upon a foundation of love, you will be proud of the fruits that have blossomed from the roots you have been tending to. Be patient and consistent, and you will pretty soon be rewarded.

Do something today that gives you peace. Take a long, warm shower, step outside, scribble or paint, or why not connect to a loved one. One little step is also you need to make and experience a shift.

Release, release something from your mind, body and soul that serves no good purpose to you any longer. Release your fear of the unknown and instead, believe in the moment and live it to the best.

Meditation, that's your answer. Sit down every morning and evening for 15 minutes each. Find a Hari Om meditation online. Meditate along the chants. Do this for 21 days and feel the change you have been missing.

FEB 1 8 2017

Start Journaling. You need clarity of thoughts. Maintaining a journal would help you bring in that clarity. Write down your thoughts, whatever that bothers you, small or big. Just release it from your heart. Practicing this regularly would provide you a lot of clarity and ease.

Colors. You need to add more colors in your daily life. Now that can be a bright phone wallpaper, colorful curtain, bedsheets around you. Bring color to your wardrobe the next time you shop. This doesn't mean that you have to spend a fortune on it. Just little things here and there, and a lot of color on them.

Discipline. You need discipline right now. Specifically for your own self, your body and soul. You have been ignoring yourself quite a bit off late. Pull up your socks, and bring discipline for yourself. Taking care of others is not the only thing that matters. You need to do things for yourself too. And for that there needs to be some discipline.

CALM AND CENTERED

Get off the screen now. You need an online detox. Give yourself a 24-hour break from social media, screens or any gadget. Relax and spend time with yourself. Sleep a little more and make the most out of this break time you earned.

Why don't you sit with yourself today? Talk to self, understand what's going on, what is needed that will feed your soul and give you peace? Sit in quiet and listen to what is calling your attention.

Past is gone, the future is uncertain, why are you so involved in both? Live in the moment, rejoice in the present, thank lord for the breath you are taking. Lucky are the ones who live in the grace of lord all time.

Close your eyes, take a deep breath and relax. Focus on your breathing. Inhale slowly, exhale slowly. Everything is in harmony, everything is in sync. Inhale again, hold, exhale slowly. Repeat.

Eli

Forgive someone today. Someone who hurt you, someone who didn't meet your expectations, someone who misunderstood you, just forgive them. Stop carrying the burden and let it go. Free yourself from those emotions, just for yourself. That is the first move of self love.

IF you are feeling stuck, unable to move or take decisions, everything is cluttered in head, it is time to move out, yes you are reading it right, move your body, go out and meet people, talk to them and exchange...exchange a smile, a conversation, something they need that you have and watch yourself move forward.

One step at a time. Don't overburden yourself with so many activities and tasks. You won't be able to be at ease otherwise.

Balance your outer and inner self. Weigh the tasks before you start them. Sometimes things are good on the face of it however they don't give inner peace. And then, it becomes a vicious circle of stress and discomfort.

It's time to get creative. Set on some adventurous trip metaphorically. Pick up a lost hobby or a new interest and let your creative juices flow. It's going to rejuvenate you.

Do not get influenced by rumors unless you see the face of it. Do not indulge in gossip. What we see is often different from what we hear. Be wise.

Light an Orange candle and meditate near it for sometime. Do this for 11 days and see the changes. Keep a glass of water before you start meditating. And drink it sip by sip post your meditation.

Stand in front of the mirror. Do you not see beauty? Beautiful lips, eyes, and so much more to be grateful for. Why do you crib about not feeling good about your looks? You are very beautiful. See you are radiating.

What is life? Have you found the answer? Well, no one has. So, live, experience, enjoy and be a source of happiness for many. You will find joy in life.

Challenge yourself Now. You are capable of much more.

It's all going in the right direction. Why worry unnecessarily?

For the next 11 days, go to a garden/park, walk at a medium pace and see children playing. Their playfulness and innocence will make you feel come back to life again.

Walk barefoot on the grass every morning for the next 5 days. While you walk, take out 2-4 minutes to just stand and be on the grass. Close your eyes and feel the nourishment it is providing to your soul.

Move yourself, Create some action. Walk, exercise, do some yoga, whatever you want. But shake yourself up a bit, you need that so much right now. Not to just lose weight but to lose the negativity.

Open an old photo album today and feel nostalgic. Bring back some old memories today but smile at them, don't be sad about them. Smile that you have been able to look back at memories. Be grateful.

Use some paints and paper to unblock your energy. Draw, color, create what you are feeling. Release it through colors.

Make way for your transformation. Nothing is stopping you, it's just you.The moment you feel you are in a cocoon, think about the caterpillar and the butterfly. That's the metamorphosis you can create in your life too.

Look at the sky, it is so vast, it's infinite. That is exactly how your potential is, it's infinite. All you need to do is, tap into it today. Sit with yourself, give yourself time and tap into your hidden, unexplored potential.

When was the last time you had a meal without distractions? Make a rule this week, you will eat without distractions. If you think you'll need to adjust the time of your meal to have no distraction, be it. Enjoy every morsel of your food. And see the shift of energy in your body.

Invoke the fire in you. There is so much light and energy in you. Just give yourself a chance and look within. Passion is what you need. Invoke a passion that you have been resisting for a while now.

Have you been able to make yourself happy? Then why are you bothered about someone being unhappy because of you. Firstly, make yourself happy and everything is secondary.

You want to cry, so cry. Let it all out with all your willpower. Now, after you are done crying, feel the sigh of relief. Feel it so deep within you. Now relax your breath and start afresh.

Peep outside from a window. Just see how everything changes but it doesn't. Now look at the same thing without the window in the middle. Isn't everything still the same? Just a different perspective!

Immerse yourself in the moonlight. Sit under the moonlight and feel calm. Let it fix that for you which you aren't able to. If there is no moon, find a moon meditation,close your eyes and feel the moonlight with the help of a meditation.

breathe

Find yourself a wall clock or a simple alarm clock would also do. Stare at it for one minute and observe your breath getting relaxed with every few seconds. Don't breathe in a haste to compete with the second hand. Instead, relax it with every passing second.

Protect
your
energy

Spend the next 48 hours without complaining about anything. Observe, become aware the moment you are about to crib or complain, and stop yourself right there. Repeat this activity every week and see the changes it brings in your life.

Have a question? Close your eyes, think about the question again and now seek the answer. Chances are extremely high that you can find the answers to your question, yourself. The only thing you need is awareness.

Happiness is a choice, you must have heard it, haven't you? However, have you actually chosen happiness or are you still waiting for someone else to make you happy? Common, make the choice and be happy!

pray

Pray before every meal, pray before cooking, pray before you take the first sip of water after you get up. Pray that the food you eat, the water you drink provides you peace and good health.

If you reach for the light, you are surely going to see light. But if you are persistent in reaching out for misery and confusion, probability is that you would always remain in that vicious circle. We receive what we really look out for. Try it and attract it.

Every experience is there to make things clearer for you. Gain clarity from every experience and consider it to be a learning experience. Consider that it is always sharpening your thought process. And, then this will be the beginning of your inner growth.

11:11

You charged your gadgets without forgetting. But did you charge yourself? Do you remember that if you forget to charge yourself, charging gadgets would do you no good. So, find a way to charge your inner self today. It's time to do some inner work.

Grateful

Stop talking to yourself about all the negative things that happened to you in the past. Instead talk about how you have transformed and healed in many ways. Talk about how strong you are and attract more strength from the universe.

www.ingramcontent.com/pod-product-compliance
Lightning Source LLC
LaVergne TN
LVHW021141160826
845679LV00023B/1998

9798891336230